Collage and sewing

Fingerprints and colored pencil

For my dad, mom, granddad, grandmom, auntie,
uncle, my teachers – thank you for the warm support.
For Jimmy Liao, my favorite 'Art star' from Taiwan –
thank you for being the moonlight in my life.
For Martin, Alexis, David, Leilani, Caroline, Helen,
Shiyu, Monica, Murmur partners, all dear friends,
and you, the reader – thank you for all the warm
hugs and encouragement for tiny, tiny me.

Fifi Kuo

First published in North America in 2019 by Boxer Books Limited.
www.boxerbooks.com
Boxer® is a registered trademark of Boxer Books Limited.

Text and illustrations copyright © 2019 Fifi Kuo
The right of Fifi Kuo to be identified as the author and illustrator
of this work has been asserted by her in accordance
with the Copyright, Designs and Patents Act, 1988.
All rights reserved, including the right of reproduction in whole
or in part in any form.
Library of Congress Cataloging-in-Publication Data available.
The artwork for this book was created using charcoal, colored
pencil, paint, digital color, collage and needle and thread.
The text is set in Bookshelf.

ISBN 978-1-910716-96-0
1 3 5 7 9 10 8 6 4 2
Printed in China
All of our papers are sourced from managed forests
and renewable resources.

Everyone CAN DRAW

FiFi Kuo

Boxer Books

Some people . . .
like to draw characters.

Some people . . .

like to draw scenes.

Some people . . . draw in black and white.

Some people . . . .

draw in lots of colors.

Some people . . .

draw with scissors.

Some people . . .

draw with hands, fingers, and toes.

Some people . . .

draw with a needle and thread.

Some people . . .

draw
in their
special
corner.

Some people . . .

draw in their dreams.

The most important
and wonderful thing is . . .

ENJOY

YOUR

What will you DRAW?

Collage

Felt tip pen

Colored pencil

Fingerprints

Chinese ink and paint and colored pencil